Proxy Wars: The Yemen Conflict as a Battlefield Between Iran and Saudi Arabia

Copyright Page

TITLE: Proxy Wars: The Yemen Conflict as a Battlefield Between Iran and Saudi Arabia

1ST Edition

ISBN: 9798215164136

Table of Contents

Proxy Wars: The Yemen Conflict as a Battlefield for Iran and Saudi Arabia

By Roberto Miguel Rodriguez

Chapter 1: The Yemen Civil War: A Proxy War Between Iran and Saudi Arabia

The Historical Context of the Yemen Conflict

The Yemen conflict, also known as the Yemen Civil War, has deep historical roots that have contributed to its complex nature. Understanding the historical context of this conflict is essential in comprehending the dynamics of the ongoing proxy war between Iran and Saudi Arabia.

Yemen's history is marked by tribal divisions and regional power struggles. These divisions date back centuries, with rivalries between different factions within the country. The fall of the Ottoman Empire in the early 20th century further exacerbated these divisions, leading to the creation of separate entities within Yemen.

In 1962, a revolution took place in North Yemen, leading to the establishment of the Yemen Arab Republic (YAR). Meanwhile, South Yemen gained independence from British colonial rule in 1967, forming the People's Democratic Republic of Yemen (PDRY). The ideological differences between these two states, with the YAR leaning towards a conservative Islamic ideology and the PDRY adopting a socialist stance, created tensions that would persist for years to come.

In 1990, North and South Yemen unified to form the Republic of Yemen. However, this merger failed to address the underlying divisions and power struggles within the country. The central government's authority remained weak, and regional differences persisted, leading to periodic conflicts and rebellions.

The roots of the current conflict can be traced back to the Arab Spring in 2011 when mass protests erupted across Yemen, demanding political reforms and an end to corruption. President Ali Abdullah Saleh, who had ruled Yemen for over three decades, was forced to step down in 2012, leaving a power vacuum that various factions sought to fill.

The Houthi movement, a Zaidi Shia rebel group from the north, took advantage of the power vacuum and seized control of the capital, Sana'a, in 2014. This prompted Saudi Arabia and a coalition of Sunni Arab states to intervene militarily in support of the internationally recognized Yemeni government, which had been ousted by the Houthis.

The conflict in Yemen quickly turned into a proxy war between Iran and Saudi Arabia. Iran, a predominantly Shia nation, saw an opportunity to exert influence in Yemen by supporting the Houthi rebels. Saudi Arabia, a predominantly Sunni nation and Iran's regional rival, considered the Houthi takeover a threat to its security and launched a military campaign to restore the Yemeni government.

The historical context of the Yemen conflict has had significant implications for the region and the international community. The sectarian divide between Shias and Sunnis has deepened, fueling the proxy war dynamics between Iran and Saudi Arabia. Non-state actors, such as Al-Qaeda in the Arabian Peninsula

(AQAP) and the Islamic State (ISIS), have also exploited the chaos to gain a foothold in Yemen.

The conflict has resulted in a dire humanitarian crisis, with millions of Yemenis facing food insecurity, lack of access to healthcare, and displacement. The international community has responded with various humanitarian aid initiatives, but the scale of the crisis continues to escalate.

Efforts to reach a negotiated settlement have been hindered by the deeply entrenched positions of the warring parties and the influence of religious ideologies. The media coverage and propaganda surrounding the conflict have further complicated the situation, making it difficult to establish a common understanding of the events on the ground.

In conclusion, the historical context of the Yemen conflict provides crucial insights into the complex dynamics at play. The Yemen Civil War has become a battlefield for Iran and Saudi Arabia, with regional powers exacerbating the sectarian divide and intensifying the proxy war dynamics. The impact of this conflict on Yemen's population, economy, and potential for a negotiated settlement cannot be overstated. Diplomats and politicians must recognize the historical context to effectively engage in finding a lasting solution to this devastating conflict.

The Emergence of Proxy Warfare in Yemen

Proxy Wars: The Yemen Conflict as a Battlefield for Iran and Saudi Arabia

Subchapter: The Emergence of Proxy Warfare in Yemen

Introduction:

In recent years, Yemen has become a battleground for regional powers, particularly Iran and Saudi Arabia, as they vie for influence and control in the Middle East. The ongoing civil war in Yemen has escalated into a proxy war, where these two regional powers support opposing factions, exacerbating the conflict and further destabilizing the country. This subchapter explores the emergence of proxy warfare in Yemen, shedding light on the intricacies of this complex conflict.

Historical Context:

To fully understand the emergence of proxy warfare in Yemen, it is crucial to examine the historical context. Yemen has long been a strategic location for regional powers, given its proximity to major shipping routes and its geopolitical significance. Previous conflicts and power struggles in the region have set the stage for the current proxy war, with Iran and Saudi Arabia seeking to expand their influence and control.

Proxy Dynamics:

The proxy war in Yemen is characterized by the support both Iran and Saudi Arabia provide to opposing factions. Iran backs the Houthi rebels, who have been fighting against the internationally recognized government supported by Saudi Arabia. This support includes financial aid, weapons, and training. On the other hand, Saudi Arabia leads a coalition of Arab states that provides military support to the government forces.

Impact on Yemen:

The consequences of proxy warfare in Yemen have been devastating for the country and its people. The conflict has resulted in a humanitarian crisis of immense proportions, with millions of Yemenis facing food insecurity, malnutrition, and lack of access to basic healthcare services. Additionally, the economy has been severely affected, with infrastructure destroyed and livelihoods disrupted. The conflict has also exacerbated sectarian tensions, further dividing communities and hindering prospects for a negotiated settlement.

International Response:

The international community has responded to the Yemen civil war with varying degrees of involvement. Diplomats and politicians have sought to mediate and facilitate negotiations between the warring parties. However, these efforts have been met with numerous challenges, as the proxy dynamics and competing interests of regional powers complicate the path to a peaceful resolution.

Conclusion:

The emergence of proxy warfare in Yemen has transformed the conflict into a complex and protracted struggle with significant regional and international implications. As diplomats and politicians strive to find a solution, it is crucial to understand the role of regional powers, the impact of sectarianism, and the involvement of non-state actors. Only through a comprehensive understanding of these factors can the international community effectively address the humanitarian crisis, foster economic recovery, and pave the way for a negotiated settlement that brings lasting peace to Yemen.

Chapter 2: The Role of Regional Powers in the Yemen Civil War

Saudi Arabia's Intervention in Yemen

The Yemen conflict has evolved into a significant proxy war between Iran and Saudi Arabia, two regional powers vying for influence in the Middle East. Saudi Arabia's intervention in Yemen has had far-reaching implications for the region and has drawn the attention of diplomats and politicians worldwide.

The Yemen Civil War: A Proxy War Between Iran and Saudi Arabia

The Yemen civil war has become a battleground for the broader rivalry between Iran and Saudi Arabia. Both countries are backing opposing factions in Yemen, with Saudi Arabia supporting the internationally recognized government of President Abdrabbuh Mansur Hadi and Iran providing assistance to the Houthi rebels. This proxy war has heightened tensions in the region and exacerbated the conflict in Yemen.

The Role of Regional Powers in the Yemen Civil War

The involvement of regional powers, particularly Iran and Saudi Arabia, has had a significant impact on the dynamics of the Yemen civil war. Their support for opposing factions has prolonged the conflict and hindered efforts towards a peaceful resolution. The competition for influence has further destabilized Yemen and the wider Middle East.

The Impact of Sectarianism on the Yemen Conflict

Sectarian divisions between Sunni and Shia Muslims have played a prominent role in the Yemen conflict. Saudi Arabia, a predominantly Sunni country, sees the Houthi rebels, who belong to the Zaidi Shia sect, as an extension of Iran's influence in the region. This sectarian dimension has deepened the divide and fueled the conflict.

The International Community's Response to the Yemen Civil War

The international community has been deeply concerned about the humanitarian crisis in Yemen caused by the ongoing war. Diplomats and politicians have called for an end to the conflict and have provided humanitarian aid to alleviate the suffering of the Yemeni people. However, the international response has been divided, with some countries supporting Saudi Arabia's intervention while others have criticized its actions.

The Humanitarian Crisis in Yemen Caused by the Ongoing War

The Yemen conflict has resulted in a severe humanitarian crisis, with millions of people facing food and medical shortages, displacement, and a lack of basic services. The ongoing war has devastated Yemen's infrastructure and economy, leaving the population vulnerable and in dire need of assistance. The international community must prioritize addressing the humanitarian needs of the Yemeni people and work towards a sustainable solution to the conflict.

The Role of Non-State Actors in the Yemen Civil War

Non-state actors, such as extremist groups like Al-Qaeda in the Arabian Peninsula (AQAP), have taken advantage of the chaos in Yemen to expand their influence. These groups pose a threat to regional security and complicate efforts to bring stability to the country. Addressing the presence of non-state actors is crucial in resolving the Yemen conflict.

The Economic Consequences of the Yemen Conflict

The Yemen conflict has had severe economic consequences for the country, leading to a sharp decline in GDP, widespread unemployment, and a collapse of essential services. The war has hindered Yemen's development and made it one of the world's poorest countries. Rebuilding Yemen's economy will require significant investment and sustained efforts to restore stability.

The Proxy War Dynamics Between Iran and Saudi Arabia in Yemen

Iran and Saudi Arabia's proxy war in Yemen has added another layer of complexity to the conflict. Their rivalry has prolonged the war and made it difficult to achieve a negotiated settlement. Diplomats and politicians must work towards de-escalation and finding a political solution that addresses the concerns of both regional powers.

The Influence of Religious Ideologies on the Yemen Civil War

Religious ideologies, particularly Sunni and Shia interpretations of Islam, have influenced the Yemen civil war. The conflict has been framed as a sectarian struggle, fueling divisions and making it harder to bridge the gap between opposing factions.

Diplomatic efforts should focus on promoting inclusivity and unity among Yemenis, regardless of their religious beliefs.

The Media Coverage and Propaganda in the Yemen Conflict

The media coverage of the Yemen conflict has been instrumental in shaping public opinion and influencing diplomatic efforts. Both Iran and Saudi Arabia have utilized propaganda to advance their narratives and gain support for their respective causes. Diplomats and politicians must critically analyze media reports and ensure that accurate information is disseminated to promote a better understanding of the conflict.

The Potential for a Negotiated Settlement in the Yemen Civil War

Despite the complexities of the Yemen conflict, there is still potential for a negotiated settlement. Diplomats and politicians must prioritize diplomacy and engage all relevant stakeholders to find a political solution that addresses the root causes of the conflict. A negotiated settlement would not only bring an end to the suffering of the Yemeni people but also contribute to regional stability and security.

Iran's Support for the Houthi Rebels

Subchapter: Iran's Support for the Houthi Rebels

Introduction:

As the Yemen Civil War rages on, it has become increasingly evident that the conflict serves as a battleground for regional powers, particularly Iran and Saudi Arabia. This subchapter focuses on Iran's support for the Houthi rebels, shedding light on the complex proxy war dynamics at play in Yemen. Addressing diplomats and politicians, it aims to provide a comprehensive understanding of Iran's role in the conflict, its motivations, and the implications it has for regional stability and the potential for a negotiated settlement.

Iran's Motivations:

Iran's support for the Houthi rebels can be attributed to a mix of strategic, ideological, and sectarian factors. Tehran views Yemen as an important arena to counter Saudi influence and expand its regional footprint. By backing the Houthi rebels, Iran seeks to challenge Saudi Arabia's dominance and gain leverage in the wider region. Moreover, the Houthis' Zaidi Shia background aligns with Iran's Shia-centric foreign policy, making them a natural ally in its broader sectarian struggle against Sunni powers.

Military Support and Proxy Warfare:

Iran's support for the Houthi rebels has included the provision of arms, training, and financial aid, enabling the Houthis to sustain their insurgency. This assistance has allowed the rebels to launch frequent cross-border attacks into Saudi Arabia, destabilizing the region further. The use of proxy warfare tactics by Iran in Yemen underscores its wider strategy of using non-state actors to advance its regional objectives while maintaining plausible deniability.

Implications for Regional Stability:

The conflict in Yemen, fueled by Iran's support for the Houthis, has exacerbated tensions between Iran and Saudi Arabia, threatening to escalate into a larger regional confrontation. The involvement of these two major regional powers has also contributed to the sectarian divide, intensifying the Sunni-Shia fault lines across the Middle East. This subchapter delves into the impact of sectarianism on the Yemen conflict, emphasizing the need for a comprehensive diplomatic approach to mitigate further escalation and restore stability.

The Potential for a Negotiated Settlement:

While the conflict in Yemen has proven to be highly complex, a negotiated settlement remains the most viable path towards ending the violence and addressing the humanitarian crisis. Understanding Iran's support for the Houthi rebels is key to facilitating a meaningful dialogue between the warring parties. This subchapter explores the potential for a negotiated settlement, highlighting the importance of engaging all relevant stakeholders, including Iran, in the peace process.

Conclusion:

Iran's support for the Houthi rebels has played a significant role in fueling the Yemen Civil War, turning it into a proxy battleground for regional powers. By delving into Iran's motivations, military support, and the implications it has for regional stability, this subchapter provides diplomats and politicians with essential insights into the complex dynamics of the conflict. It underscores the urgency of finding a negotiated settlement to end the violence and alleviate the humanitarian crisis, urging the international community to engage all relevant actors, including Iran, in the pursuit of lasting peace in Yemen.

Chapter 3: The Impact of Sectarianism on the Yemen Conflict

The Sunni-Shia Divide in Yemen

The Yemen conflict, often referred to as a proxy war between Iran and Saudi Arabia, is deeply rooted in the Sunni-Shia divide that has plagued the country for years. This subchapter aims to explore the impact of this sectarian divide on the ongoing conflict, shedding light on its historical context, religious ideologies, and its role in shaping the dynamics of the proxy war.

Yemen, a predominantly Sunni country, has long been marked by tensions between its Sunni majority and the Shia minority known as the Houthis. The divide escalated in 2014 when the Houthis, backed by Iran, seized control of the capital, Sanaa, and other major cities. This triggered a military intervention by a Saudi-led coalition, in support of the internationally recognized government, which is predominantly Sunni.

The sectarian nature of the conflict has intensified as both Iran and Saudi Arabia use their religious ideologies to mobilize support and influence the warring factions. Iran, a Shia-majority country, sees the Houthis as a strategic ally in the region, aiming to expand its influence and counter Saudi Arabia's power. On the other hand, Saudi Arabia views the conflict as a matter of defending the Sunni community and preventing Iran from gaining a foothold in the Arabian Peninsula.

The Sunni-Shia divide in Yemen has further complicated the proxy war dynamics between Iran and Saudi Arabia. Both regional powers have been providing military and financial support to their respective proxies, exacerbating the violence and prolonging the conflict. This has created a complex web of alliances and rivalries, with non-state actors such as Al-Qaeda and ISIS also exploiting the sectarian tensions to further their own agendas.

The impact of this divide goes beyond the battlefield, as it has exacerbated the already dire humanitarian crisis in Yemen. The ongoing war has led to widespread displacement, food insecurity, and a collapsing healthcare system, leaving millions of Yemenis in urgent need of assistance. The international community, including diplomats and politicians, has struggled to effectively respond to the crisis, with efforts for a negotiated settlement often hindered by the deep-rooted sectarian tensions.

In conclusion, the Sunni-Shia divide in Yemen has played a significant role in shaping the dynamics of the proxy war between Iran and Saudi Arabia. The historical context, religious ideologies, and the involvement of regional powers have perpetuated the conflict and worsened the humanitarian crisis. Diplomats and politicians must recognize the complex sectarian dynamics at play and work towards a negotiated settlement that addresses the root causes of the conflict, with the ultimate goal of restoring peace and stability in Yemen.

Sectarian Narrative and Recruitment Strategies

The Yemen Civil War has been deeply influenced by sectarian narratives and recruitment strategies employed by both Iran and Saudi Arabia. This subchapter delves into the tactics utilized by these regional powers to fuel the conflict and recruit fighters to their respective causes.

Throughout the Yemen Civil War, both Iran and Saudi Arabia have actively promoted sectarian narratives to justify their involvement and gain support from their own populations and the wider Muslim world. Iran, a predominantly Shia country, has portrayed itself as the defender of Shia communities in Yemen, arguing that it is their religious duty to support their fellow Shias against the Sunni-led government. On the other hand, Saudi Arabia, a predominantly Sunni country, has framed its intervention as a defense against Iranian influence and expansionism, presenting itself as the protector of Sunni interests in the region.

These sectarian narratives have had a significant impact on the conflict, exacerbating existing divisions and escalating violence. They have fueled sectarian tensions within Yemen, leading to increased polarization and radicalization among the population. As a result, recruitment strategies deployed by both Iran and Saudi Arabia have been effective in mobilizing fighters to join their respective sides.

Iran has utilized its extensive network of proxies, such as the Houthi rebels, to recruit fighters and expand its influence in Yemen. It has provided military support, funding, and training to these groups, attracting individuals who share a sense of religious duty and allegiance to the Shia cause. Saudi Arabia, on the other hand, has formed alliances with various Sunni militias, offering financial incentives and military assistance to recruit fighters who align with their anti-Iran narrative.

The role of non-state actors in the Yemen Civil War cannot be overlooked. These groups, influenced by sectarian ideologies and driven by their own agendas, have contributed to the escalation of the conflict. They have been instrumental in recruiting fighters, exacerbating sectarian tensions, and prolonging the war.

The impact of sectarian narratives and recruitment strategies goes beyond the borders of Yemen. It has created a proxy war dynamic between Iran and Saudi Arabia, with both countries using Yemen as a battlefield to assert their regional influence. The international community has responded to this conflict with mixed reactions, often divided along sectarian lines themselves, further hindering efforts to find a negotiated settlement.

In conclusion, the sectarian narrative and recruitment strategies employed by Iran and Saudi Arabia have played a significant role in the Yemen Civil War. These tactics have intensified sectarian divisions, fueled violence, and hindered efforts towards a peaceful resolution. Diplomats and politicians must recognize and address these factors to effectively contribute to a sustainable and inclusive peace process in Yemen.

Chapter 4: The International Community's Response to the Yemen Civil War

United Nations' Efforts for Peace in Yemen

The ongoing conflict in Yemen has been a source of immense suffering for the Yemeni people, with devastating consequences for their lives, livelihoods, and future prospects. The United Nations (UN) has been at the forefront of international efforts to bring about peace and stability in Yemen, recognizing the urgent need for a negotiated settlement to end the violence and address the humanitarian crisis.

The UN's role in Yemen has been multifaceted, encompassing diplomatic, humanitarian, and peacekeeping initiatives. Diplomatically, the UN has been actively engaged in facilitating negotiations and dialogue between the warring parties, with the aim of reaching a comprehensive and inclusive peace agreement. The UN Special Envoy for Yemen has been tirelessly working to bring all stakeholders to the table and find common ground for a sustainable political solution.

In addition to diplomatic efforts, the UN has been instrumental in providing vital humanitarian assistance to the Yemeni people. The conflict has had a devastating impact on Yemen's civilian population, leading to widespread food insecurity, a collapse of healthcare services, and a dire humanitarian crisis. The UN, through its agencies and partners, has been actively delivering aid, providing medical assistance, and supporting the most vulnerable communities in Yemen.

Furthermore, the UN has been closely monitoring and documenting human rights abuses committed during the conflict, ensuring that perpetrators are held accountable for their actions. The UN Human Rights Council has established a Group of Eminent Experts on Yemen, tasked with investigating and reporting on human rights violations, including those that may amount to war crimes.

While the UN's efforts have been commendable, the path to peace in Yemen remains challenging. The conflict is deeply rooted in regional power struggles and sectarian tensions, with Iran and Saudi Arabia backing opposing factions. Non-state actors, such as Houthi rebels and terrorist groups, further complicate the dynamics on the ground.

Despite these complexities, the UN continues to advocate for a negotiated settlement, urging all parties to cease hostilities and engage in meaningful dialogue. The international community, including diplomats and politicians, must support these efforts and work towards a sustainable peace in Yemen. It is crucial to address the root causes of the conflict, including the impact of sectarianism and religious ideologies, while also addressing the economic consequences and media coverage that perpetuate the violence.

Ultimately, a negotiated settlement is the most viable path to peace in Yemen. The UN's efforts, combined with the support of regional powers and the international community, offer hope for a resolution to the conflict and an end to the humanitarian crisis in Yemen. Diplomats and politicians must seize this opportunity and actively engage in the pursuit of peace, ensuring a brighter and more stable future for the people of Yemen.

Role of the United States, United Kingdom, and France

In the complex and volatile landscape of the Yemen Civil War, the involvement of global powers such as the United States, United Kingdom, and France has played a crucial role. These nations, with their extensive diplomatic and military capabilities, have exerted a significant influence on the conflict, shaping its dynamics and outcomes.

From the outset, the United States has been deeply involved in the Yemen conflict, primarily supporting the Saudi-led coalition. With a vested interest in countering Iranian influence in the region, the US has provided extensive military assistance, including arms sales, intelligence sharing, and logistical support to its Saudi allies. Moreover, the US has conducted drone strikes targeting Al-Qaeda in the Arabian Peninsula (AQAP) and ISIS in Yemen, further complicating the conflict.

The United Kingdom, historically close to Saudi Arabia, has similarly aligned itself with the Saudi-led coalition. Besides providing military support, including arms sales, the UK has been involved in training Saudi forces and offering diplomatic backing. However, the UK's role has faced significant criticism due to allegations of human rights violations by Saudi forces in Yemen.

France, too, has been an active player in the Yemen conflict. While not directly involved in the military operations, France has supplied arms to Saudi Arabia and the United Arab Emirates, contributing to their military capabilities. Additionally, France has been engaged in diplomatic efforts to find a political solution to the conflict, participating in peace talks and advocating for a negotiated settlement.

The involvement of these global powers has had profound implications for the Yemen conflict. Their support has bolstered the military capabilities of the Saudi-led coalition, enabling it to sustain its operations against Houthi rebels. However, their backing has also drawn criticism, as the conflict has resulted in a severe humanitarian crisis, with widespread civilian casualties and a dire shortage of essential supplies.

Furthermore, the role of the United States, United Kingdom, and France has exacerbated the sectarian tensions underlying the Yemen conflict. The perception of these powers aligning with Sunni-majority Saudi Arabia against the Shia Houthi rebels has deepened the sectarian divide, fueling a sense of marginalization and animosity among the Houthi population.

As diplomats and politicians navigate the complexities of the Yemen Civil War, understanding the role of these global powers is crucial. Their actions and policies have shaped the conflict, influenced the international response, and determined the outcome of the proxy war between Iran and Saudi Arabia. Moving forward, it is essential for these nations to reassess their involvement and prioritize a negotiated settlement that addresses the humanitarian crisis and promotes stability in Yemen.

Chapter 5: The Humanitarian Crisis in Yemen Caused by the Ongoing War

The Devastating Effects of the Conflict on Yemeni Civilians

As the Yemen conflict continues to escalate, the devastating effects on Yemeni civilians cannot be ignored. This subchapter delves into the immense toll the war has taken on innocent lives, shedding light on the urgent need for diplomatic and political intervention.

The Yemen Civil War: A Proxy War Between Iran and Saudi Arabia

The ongoing conflict in Yemen serves as a proxy war between regional powers Iran and Saudi Arabia. Unfortunately, it is the Yemeni civilians who bear the brunt of this power struggle. The indiscriminate bombings, blockades, and fighting have resulted in a staggering number of casualties and displacement.

The Impact of Sectarianism on the Yemen Conflict

Sectarian tensions have exacerbated the Yemen conflict, deepening the divide between different religious and ethnic groups. This has led to increased violence and the targeting of civilians based solely on their religious affiliation. The cycle of revenge and retaliation has added fuel to an already volatile situation.

The Humanitarian Crisis in Yemen Caused by the Ongoing War

The Yemen conflict has given rise to one of the worst humanitarian crises in recent history. The constant airstrikes, destruction of infrastructure, and blockades have severely limited access to food, water, and healthcare for millions of Yemeni civilians. Malnutrition and disease are rampant, with children being the most vulnerable victims.

The International Community's Response to the Yemen Civil War

The international community's response to the Yemen conflict has been mixed. While some countries have provided humanitarian aid and condemned the violence, others have been complicit in fueling the conflict through arms sales and political support. Diplomats and politicians must unite to find a collective solution that prioritizes the well-being of Yemeni civilians over geopolitical interests.

The Role of Non-State Actors in the Yemen Civil War

Non-state actors, such as Houthi rebels and terrorist organizations, have further complicated the Yemen conflict. Their involvement has perpetuated violence and hindered efforts for a peaceful resolution. Diplomatic efforts should aim to mitigate the influence of these actors and bring them to the negotiating table.

The Economic Consequences of the Yemen Conflict

The Yemen conflict has caused severe economic devastation, with the country's infrastructure in shambles and its economy in ruins. The destruction of vital industries and the disruption of trade have resulted in widespread poverty and unemployment. A comprehensive plan for post-conflict reconstruction and economic recovery is essential to alleviate the suffering of Yemeni civilians.

The Potential for a Negotiated Settlement in the Yemen Civil War

Despite the grim situation, there is still potential for a negotiated settlement in the Yemen Civil War. Diplomats and politicians must engage in sustained dialogue, leveraging the influence of regional powers to broker peace. This subchapter explores the various obstacles and opportunities for a political resolution that prioritizes the needs and rights of Yemeni civilians.

In conclusion, the devastating effects of the Yemen conflict on civilians cannot be underestimated. Diplomats and politicians must address the urgent humanitarian crisis and work towards a negotiated settlement that brings an end to the suffering of innocent Yemeni men, women, and children. Only through concerted international efforts can the Yemeni people begin to rebuild their lives and their country.

Displacement, Food Insecurity, and Disease Outbreaks

In the midst of the Yemen Civil War, the consequences of conflict extend far beyond the battlefield. Displacement, food insecurity, and disease outbreaks have become intertwined issues that exacerbate the already dire situation on the ground. As diplomats and politicians, it is crucial to understand the complex interplay between these factors and their implications for the ongoing conflict.

One of the most alarming consequences of the Yemen Civil War is the mass displacement of civilians. The conflict has uprooted millions of Yemenis from their homes, forcing them to seek refuge in overcrowded camps or flee to neighboring countries. This displacement not only disrupts the lives of individuals and families but also puts an immense strain on host communities, exacerbating existing tensions and potentially fueling further conflict.

The displacement crisis has also led to a severe food insecurity situation in Yemen. The war has disrupted agricultural activities, decimated livestock, and destroyed critical infrastructure, leaving millions of Yemenis without access to adequate food and water. As a result, malnutrition rates have soared, particularly among children, leading to a humanitarian catastrophe of unprecedented proportions.

Moreover, the breakdown of healthcare systems due to the conflict has created fertile ground for disease outbreaks. Yemen is currently grappling with one of the world's worst cholera epidemics, as well as outbreaks of other infectious diseases such as diphtheria and measles. The lack of proper sanitation, clean water, and medical supplies further compounds the crisis, leaving Yemenis vulnerable to preventable and treatable diseases.

Addressing the displacement, food insecurity, and disease outbreaks in Yemen requires a comprehensive and multi-faceted approach. Diplomats and politicians must prioritize the protection of civilians and ensure the provision of humanitarian aid to those in need. This includes supporting organizations on the ground that are working tirelessly to provide food, clean water, and medical assistance.

Furthermore, efforts should be made to promote a negotiated settlement to the conflict, as a sustainable peace agreement would be the most effective way to alleviate the suffering of the Yemeni people. Regional powers, such as Iran and Saudi Arabia, must recognize the devastating consequences of their proxy war and work towards a resolution that prioritizes the well-being of Yemeni civilians above all else.

In conclusion, the displacement, food insecurity, and disease outbreaks resulting from the Yemen Civil War are critical issues that demand urgent attention. The impact of these factors extends far beyond the immediate conflict zone, affecting the lives of millions of Yemenis and exacerbating an already dire humanitarian crisis. As diplomats and politicians, it is our responsibility to work towards a peaceful resolution that addresses these pressing issues and brings much-needed relief to the Yemeni people.

Chapter 6: The Role of Non-State Actors in the Yemen Civil War

Houthi Rebels and Their Ideology

The Houthi rebels, also known as Ansar Allah, have played a significant role in the Yemen Civil War, which is widely regarded as a proxy war between Iran and Saudi Arabia. Understanding the ideology of the Houthi rebels is crucial for diplomats and politicians engaged in resolving the conflict and for comprehending the dynamics of the war.

The Houthi rebels adhere to a unique branch of Shia Islam known as Zaidism. Zaidism is a moderate form of Shia Islam that originated in Yemen and is distinct from the Twelver Shia Islam practiced in Iran. The Houthi rebels draw inspiration from Zaidi teachings and believe in the restoration of the Zaidi Imamate, a historical political system that provided leadership to Yemeni Zaidis for over a thousand years.

However, the Houthi rebels' ideology has evolved over time, becoming increasingly radicalized. This shift can be attributed to a combination of factors, including political marginalization, economic grievances, and external influences. Iran has been accused of providing financial, military, and ideological support to the Houthi rebels, exacerbating their radicalization and strengthening their resolve to challenge the Saudi-backed government.

The Houthi rebels' ideology has also been influenced by regional power dynamics and sectarianism. As Iran and Saudi Arabia vie for dominance in the region, Yemen has become a battleground for their proxy war. The Houthi rebels, with their Zaidi background, have found common cause with Iran, which champions the Shia cause, further fueling their conflict with the Saudi-backed government and Sunni-majority Yemen.

The Houthi rebels' ideology has also had a profound impact on the Yemeni society and the ongoing humanitarian crisis. Their pursuit of power and control has resulted in widespread violence, displacement, and a severe humanitarian catastrophe. The international community has responded to the crisis through aid and diplomatic efforts, but a negotiated settlement remains elusive due to the complex ideological underpinnings of the conflict.

In conclusion, understanding the ideology of the Houthi rebels is essential for diplomats and politicians seeking to resolve the Yemen Civil War. Their adherence to Zaidism, radicalization over time, and external influences have all contributed to their role in the proxy war between Iran and Saudi Arabia. The impact of their ideology on Yemeni society, the humanitarian crisis, and the potential for a negotiated settlement cannot be underestimated.

Al-Qaeda and ISIS in Yemen

The presence of Al-Qaeda and ISIS in Yemen has added another layer of complexity to the ongoing Yemen Civil War, which is primarily a proxy war between Iran and Saudi Arabia. This subchapter will delve into the role of these non-state actors in the conflict and the implications it has for regional powers, the international community, and the potential for a negotiated settlement.

Both Al-Qaeda and ISIS have taken advantage of the chaos and power vacuum created by the civil war to establish strongholds in various parts of Yemen. Al-Qaeda in the Arabian Peninsula (AQAP) has been particularly active, exploiting sectarian tensions and tribal rivalries to expand its influence. This poses a significant challenge for both Iran and Saudi Arabia, as they try to maintain control over their respective proxies while combatting the threat posed by these extremist groups.

For regional powers, the presence of Al-Qaeda and ISIS further complicates their involvement in the Yemen conflict. While Iran and Saudi Arabia have been supporting opposing factions, both have a shared interest in combating these terrorist organizations. However, their divergent approaches and priorities have hindered effective collaboration, leaving Yemen vulnerable to continued terrorist activities.

The international community has also been concerned about the rise of Al-Qaeda and ISIS in Yemen. These groups not only pose a threat to regional stability but also have the potential to conduct attacks globally. Diplomats and politicians must recognize the urgent need for a coordinated response, including intelligence sharing, counterterrorism efforts, and addressing the root causes of extremism in Yemen.

Furthermore, the presence of non-state actors like Al-Qaeda and ISIS exacerbates the humanitarian crisis in Yemen. Their activities have resulted in the displacement of thousands of

Yemenis and further limited access to humanitarian aid. This calls for increased international assistance and efforts to address the underlying causes of the conflict.

While the focus of the Yemen Civil War has primarily been on the proxy war dynamics between Iran and Saudi Arabia, the presence of Al-Qaeda and ISIS cannot be overlooked. Their influence, driven by religious ideologies and the power vacuum in Yemen, has far-reaching consequences for regional stability and global security. Diplomats and politicians must prioritize addressing this threat and work towards a negotiated settlement that not only brings an end to the civil war but also ensures the eradication of extremist groups in Yemen.

Chapter 7: The Economic Consequences of the Yemen Conflict

Destruction of Infrastructure and Economic Institutions

The Yemen Civil War has been marked by the destruction of infrastructure and economic institutions, resulting in severe damage to the country's economy and hindering its development. This subchapter will explore the devastating consequences of the conflict on Yemen's infrastructure and economic institutions, shedding light on the urgent need for reconstruction efforts and economic stability.

The ongoing war between Iran and Saudi Arabia in Yemen has taken a heavy toll on the country's infrastructure. Key infrastructure such as roads, bridges, airports, and ports have been targeted and destroyed, making it difficult for humanitarian aid and essential supplies to reach the affected population. This has resulted in a humanitarian crisis, with millions of Yemenis suffering from food and medicine shortages, lack of clean water, and inadequate healthcare.

Moreover, the conflict has also targeted economic institutions, further exacerbating the economic crisis in Yemen. Banks, factories, and businesses have been destroyed, leading to widespread unemployment and economic instability. The destruction of Yemen's economic infrastructure has had a long-lasting impact, as it will take significant time and resources to rebuild and revive the economy.

The destruction of infrastructure and economic institutions in Yemen has not only affected the country's internal dynamics but has also had regional implications. As a proxy war between Iran and Saudi Arabia, the conflict has disrupted trade and economic ties between Yemen and its neighboring countries. The instability in Yemen has also had a negative impact on regional stability, with the potential for spillover effects and increased tensions in the region.

Addressing the destruction of infrastructure and economic institutions in Yemen requires a comprehensive approach. The international community, including diplomats and politicians, must work together to support reconstruction efforts and provide humanitarian aid to the affected population. Efforts should also be made to promote economic stability and encourage investment in Yemen, in order to revive the country's economy and create employment opportunities.

Furthermore, a negotiated settlement that addresses the root causes of the conflict is crucial for long-term peace and stability in Yemen. This will require diplomatic efforts and engagement with all relevant stakeholders, including regional powers and non-state actors. Only through a comprehensive and inclusive approach can Yemen rebuild its infrastructure and economic institutions, paving the way for a brighter future for its people.

Impacts on Trade, Oil, and Economy of the Region

The Yemen conflict has had far-reaching impacts on the trade, oil, and economy of the region. As one of the poorest countries in the Middle East, Yemen's economy heavily relies on trade and its oil industry. However, the ongoing civil war has disrupted these sectors, causing severe economic consequences not only for Yemen but also for neighboring countries and the wider region.

Trade, which is a vital lifeline for any nation, has been significantly hampered by the conflict. The war has led to the destruction of infrastructure, including ports, roads, and airports, making it difficult for goods to enter or leave the country. This has resulted in a sharp decline in imports and exports, exacerbating the already dire economic situation. The blockade imposed by the Saudi-led coalition has further stifled trade, preventing essential goods such as food, medicine, and fuel from reaching the Yemeni people.

The Yemen conflict has also had a profound impact on the region's oil industry. Yemen was once a modest oil producer, but its oil production has plummeted due to the war. Oil infrastructure has been targeted, and the ongoing instability has deterred foreign investment in the sector. This not only affects Yemen's economy but also has wider implications for global oil prices and regional energy security.

Furthermore, the economic consequences of the conflict extend beyond Yemen's borders. The neighboring countries, particularly Saudi Arabia and the United Arab Emirates, have been deeply affected. These countries have provided financial and military support to different factions in the conflict, draining their resources. The strain on their economies has forced them to divert funds from other sectors, impacting their overall economic growth and development.

The regional economy as a whole has been impacted by the slowdown of trade and the instability in Yemen. The disruption to supply chains and the decline in trade have created economic challenges for countries in the region, affecting sectors such as manufacturing, agriculture, and tourism. The economic consequences of the conflict have been compounded by the COVID-19 pandemic, further exacerbating the challenges faced by the region.

Addressing the impacts on trade, oil, and the economy of the region requires a comprehensive approach. Diplomats and politicians must work towards a negotiated settlement in the Yemen conflict to restore stability, rebuild infrastructure, and revive the economy. Regional powers, such as Iran and Saudi Arabia, need to recognize the economic costs of the proxy war and find a political solution that prioritizes the well-being of the Yemeni people and the region as a whole. The international community should also play a crucial role in supporting Yemen's economic recovery and providing humanitarian assistance to alleviate the suffering caused by the conflict.

Chapter 8: The Proxy War Dynamics Between Iran and Saudi Arabia in Yemen

Military Support and Arms Trafficking

In the context of the Yemen conflict, military support and arms trafficking have played a significant role in intensifying the proxy war between Iran and Saudi Arabia. This subchapter aims to provide an in-depth analysis of the involvement of regional powers, the impact of sectarianism, and the role of non-state actors in the conflict.

One of the key aspects of the Yemen Civil War is the extensive military support provided to both sides by regional powers. Iran has been widely accused of supplying weapons, including missiles and drones, to the Houthi rebels, who are aligned with the Shia sect. On the other hand, Saudi Arabia has received substantial military backing from the United States and other Western allies. This military support has not only fueled the conflict but also increased the level of destruction and casualties on the ground.

Arms trafficking has also played a detrimental role in prolonging the conflict. Despite the arms embargo imposed by the United Nations, weapons continue to flow into Yemen through various illicit channels. Arms smugglers take advantage of the porous borders and the ongoing chaos to supply weapons to both sides of the conflict. This arms trafficking not only perpetuates the violence but also poses a threat to regional stability by potentially arming other non-state actors.

The impact of sectarianism cannot be overlooked in the Yemen conflict. The rivalry between Sunni-majority Saudi Arabia and Shia-majority Iran has fueled a sectarian divide, with each side supporting the respective sects in Yemen. This sectarianism has exacerbated the conflict and made it even more difficult to find a negotiated settlement.

Non-state actors, such as terrorist groups and local militias, have also played a significant role in the Yemen Civil War. Al-Qaeda in the Arabian Peninsula (AQAP) and the Islamic State (ISIS) have exploited the chaos to gain a foothold in Yemen, further complicating the conflict. These non-state actors have their own interests and agendas, which often diverge from those of the main warring parties, making a negotiated settlement even more challenging.

In conclusion, military support and arms trafficking have had a profound impact on the Yemen conflict. The involvement of regional powers, the influence of sectarianism, and the role of non-state actors have all contributed to the escalation and prolongation of the proxy war between Iran and Saudi Arabia. It is crucial for diplomats and politicians to understand these dynamics in order to find a sustainable solution and alleviate the humanitarian crisis in Yemen.

Proxy Tactics and Strategies in Yemen

The Yemen Civil War has emerged as a proxy war between Iran and Saudi Arabia, with both regional powers vying for influence and control in the country. This subchapter will delve into the various tactics and strategies employed by these actors, shedding light on the complex dynamics of the conflict.

Proxy warfare is characterized by the use of third-party actors to achieve strategic goals. In Yemen, both Iran and Saudi Arabia have employed this tactic, backing local militias and rebel groups to further their agendas. Iran has provided extensive support to the Houthi rebels, including weaponry, training, and financial aid. This has allowed the rebels to challenge the internationally recognized government and gain control over significant parts of the country.

On the other hand, Saudi Arabia has formed a coalition of Arab states to support the Yemeni government and counter Iranian influence. This coalition has conducted airstrikes against Houthi targets, aiming to weaken the rebels and restore the government's control. Additionally, Saudi Arabia has provided extensive military and economic aid to its Yemeni allies, seeking to bolster their capabilities and undermine the Houthi insurgency.

The proxy war in Yemen is also heavily influenced by sectarianism, with Iran backing the predominantly Shia Houthi rebels, while Saudi Arabia supports the Sunni-led Yemeni government. This sectarian divide has exacerbated the conflict and fueled tensions in the region. Both Iran and Saudi Arabia have used religious ideologies to rally support for their respective proxies, further deepening the sectarian divide within Yemen.

The international community has responded to the Yemen Civil War through various means, including diplomatic efforts, arms embargoes, and humanitarian aid. However, the complexity of the conflict and the involvement of powerful regional actors have hindered the effectiveness of these responses. The humanitarian crisis in Yemen has reached catastrophic levels, with millions of people facing starvation, disease, and displacement as a result of the ongoing war.

Non-state actors, such as Al-Qaeda in the Arabian Peninsula (AQAP), have also played a significant role in the Yemen Civil War. AQAP has exploited the chaos and instability to expand its influence, posing a threat to regional and international security. The presence of non-state actors further complicates the conflict and makes a negotiated settlement more challenging to achieve.

The economic consequences of the Yemen conflict have been devastating. The war has disrupted trade, destroyed infrastructure, and crippled the country's economy. Yemen, once the poorest country in the Arab world, now faces widespread poverty and economic collapse.

Media coverage and propaganda have played a crucial role in shaping the narrative of the Yemen conflict. Both Iran and Saudi Arabia have utilized media outlets and social media platforms to disseminate their respective narratives, often fueling polarization and misinformation.

Despite the grim realities on the ground, there is still potential for a negotiated settlement in the Yemen Civil War. Diplomats and politicians must work towards finding common ground and addressing the root causes of the conflict. This subchapter will explore the prospects for peace and the steps that need to be taken to achieve a sustainable resolution to the Yemen crisis.

Chapter 9: The Influence of Religious Ideologies on the Yemen Civil War

Wahhabism in Saudi Arabia and Its Impact on the Conflict

Wahhabism, a fundamentalist branch of Sunni Islam, plays a crucial role in the Yemen civil war, which is often referred to as a proxy war between Iran and Saudi Arabia. Understanding the impact of Wahhabism on this conflict is essential for diplomats and politicians seeking to navigate the complexities of the Yemen civil war.

Originating in the 18th century, Wahhabism became the dominant religious ideology in Saudi Arabia, shaping the country's governance, society, and foreign policy. This ideology promotes a puritanical interpretation of Islam, emphasizing strict adherence to Islamic law and the rejection of any practices or beliefs that deviate from it. As Saudi Arabia sought to export its version of Islam, it provided financial and ideological support to various religious groups worldwide, including in Yemen.

In Yemen, the influence of Wahhabism has exacerbated sectarian tensions and deepened the divide between Sunni and Shia Muslims. The Houthi rebels, who are aligned with Iran, are predominantly Shia, while the Yemeni government, backed by Saudi Arabia, represents the Sunni majority. The Wahhabi ideology, with its inclination towards Sunni supremacy, has fueled sectarianism and contributed to the escalation of the conflict.

Furthermore, the spread of Wahhabism in Yemen has led to the rise of non-state actors, such as Al-Qaeda in the Arabian Peninsula (AQAP) and the Islamic State (IS). These extremist groups exploit the grievances of marginalized communities and employ a distorted interpretation of Wahhabi teachings to recruit fighters and expand their influence. Their presence further complicates the conflict and poses a threat to regional security.

The international community's response to the Yemen civil war has been mixed. While some nations have supported Saudi Arabia's intervention, others have criticized its military campaign and the humanitarian crisis it has caused. The impact of Wahhabism on the conflict adds another layer of complexity to international efforts to broker a negotiated settlement. Understanding the religious dynamics at play is crucial for diplomats and politicians seeking to find common ground and facilitate peace talks.

Addressing the impact of Wahhabism on the Yemen civil war requires a comprehensive approach. This includes not only addressing the immediate security concerns but also addressing the root causes of the conflict, such as sectarian tensions and socioeconomic disparities. A holistic approach that takes into account the influence of religious ideologies, including Wahhabism, is necessary for achieving a lasting resolution to the Yemen civil war.

Zaydi Shia Islam and Its Role in the Houthi Movement

The Zaydi Shia Islam, a branch of Shia Islam with its unique theological and political beliefs, has played a crucial role in shaping the Houthi movement in Yemen. Understanding the ideological underpinnings of the Houthi rebels is essential in comprehending the dynamics of the Yemen civil war, which has become a proxy battleground for regional powers, namely Iran and Saudi Arabia.

The Houthi movement, also known as Ansar Allah, emerged in the early 1990s as a response to political and economic marginalization of Zaydi Shia Muslims in Yemen. Zaydis historically held a dominant position in Yemen's religious and political landscape, but their influence declined with the establishment of the Republic of Yemen in 1990. The Houthi movement aimed to restore Zaydi power and defend the rights of Zaydis against perceived discrimination by the Yemeni government.

The Zaydi Shia Islam differs from the Twelver Shia Islam predominant in Iran, which makes the Houthi movement unique in its theological orientation. However, Iran has provided ideological and material support to the Houthis, capitalizing on the shared Shia identity and seeking to expand its influence in the region. This support has intensified the perception of the Yemen civil war as a proxy war between Iran and Saudi Arabia, further exacerbating sectarian tensions in Yemen.

The Houthi movement's religious ideologies have also contributed to the sectarian dynamics of the conflict. The Houthi rebels view themselves as defenders of Zaydi Shia Islam against the encroachment of Sunni Islam, particularly the Saudi-backed Salafism. This perception has fueled sectarian divisions and deepened animosity between different religious groups in Yemen.

The international community's response to the Yemen civil war has been multifaceted, with various diplomatic efforts aimed at resolving the conflict. However, the complexity of the conflict, coupled with the involvement of multiple regional actors, has hindered the prospects of a negotiated settlement. The influence of religious ideologies, including the Zaydi Shia Islam, has further complicated the path to peace.

In conclusion, the Zaydi Shia Islam has played a significant role in shaping the Houthi movement and the Yemen civil war. Its distinctive religious and political beliefs have not only fueled the conflict but have also attracted the attention of regional actors such as Iran and Saudi Arabia. Understanding the role of Zaydi Shia Islam is crucial for diplomats and politicians seeking to navigate the complexities of the Yemen conflict and explore potential avenues for a negotiated settlement.

Chapter 10: The Media Coverage and Propaganda in the Yemen Conflict

The Role of Media Outlets in Shaping Public Opinion

In the ongoing Yemen Civil War, media outlets play a crucial role in shaping public opinion both domestically and internationally. As diplomats and politicians seek to understand the complexities of this proxy war between Iran and Saudi Arabia, it is essential to recognize the influence of media in molding public perception.

Media outlets, whether traditional or social, have the power to shape narratives, control information flow, and influence public opinion. In the context of the Yemen conflict, the media plays a significant role in how the war is portrayed and understood by various audiences.

Firstly, media outlets have the ability to highlight the role of regional powers in the Yemen Civil War. They can shed light on the geopolitical dynamics and interests of Iran and Saudi Arabia in the region. By analyzing their involvement, diplomats and politicians can better understand the motivations behind their actions and potentially find avenues for negotiation.

Secondly, media coverage can also emphasize the impact of sectarianism on the Yemen conflict. The media can explore how religious differences contribute to the escalation of violence and the polarization of society. This understanding is crucial for diplomats and politicians to address the root causes of the conflict and work towards reconciliation.

Another aspect that media outlets can address is the response of the international community to the Yemen Civil War. By examining the actions, statements, and policies of different countries, diplomats and politicians can gauge the level of support or opposition to the conflict. This analysis can inform diplomatic efforts and aid in building coalitions for peace.

Furthermore, media outlets have the responsibility to shed light on the humanitarian crisis in Yemen caused by the ongoing war. By highlighting the suffering of the Yemeni people, media can generate empathy and mobilize international support for humanitarian aid. This coverage can pressure diplomats and politicians to prioritize humanitarian efforts and work towards a swift resolution.

Moreover, media outlets can also explore the role of non-state actors in the Yemen Civil War. By examining the influence of groups such as Houthi rebels or Al-Qaeda in the Arabian Peninsula, diplomats and politicians can better understand the dynamics on the ground and develop targeted strategies to address these actors.

The economic consequences of the Yemen conflict are another area where media coverage is crucial. By analyzing the impact of the war on the Yemeni economy and the region as a whole, diplomats and politicians can assess the long-term implications and develop strategies for economic recovery and stability.

Additionally, the media plays a significant role in covering the proxy war dynamics between Iran and Saudi Arabia in Yemen. Through objective reporting, media outlets can provide insights into the strategies, alliances, and motivations of these regional powers, allowing diplomats and politicians to navigate the complexities of the conflict.

Religious ideologies also play a role in the Yemen Civil War, and media coverage can help diplomats and politicians understand the influence of these ideologies. By analyzing how different religious groups perceive the conflict, policymakers can tailor their approaches to find common ground and promote dialogue.

Furthermore, media coverage and propaganda in the Yemen conflict should be critically examined. By analyzing the biases and agendas of different media outlets, diplomats and politicians can differentiate between reliable information and propaganda. This discernment is essential for making informed decisions and understanding the perspectives of different actors involved.

Finally, media outlets can provide insight into the potential for a negotiated settlement in the Yemen Civil War. By highlighting initiatives, peace talks, and diplomatic efforts, media coverage can inform and engage diplomats and politicians in supporting peaceful resolutions.

In conclusion, media outlets play a pivotal role in shaping public opinion and understanding the complexities of the Yemen Civil War. Diplomats and politicians must recognize the influence of media in order to make informed decisions and work towards a peaceful resolution. By critically analyzing media coverage, policymakers can navigate the narratives, biases, and agendas to gain a comprehensive understanding of the conflict.

Disinformation Campaigns and Propaganda Techniques

In the complex web of the Yemen Civil War, disinformation campaigns and propaganda techniques have played a significant role in shaping the conflict and influencing its outcomes. This subchapter aims to shed light on the various strategies employed by both sides, Iran and Saudi Arabia, in their bid for supremacy in Yemen.

Disinformation campaigns have been a common tool used by regional powers, such as Iran and Saudi Arabia, to manipulate public opinion and gain support for their respective agendas. These campaigns often involve spreading false or misleading information through various channels, including social media, traditional media outlets, and even diplomatic channels. By disseminating distorted narratives and exaggerating events, these actors aim to shape public perception, garner sympathy, and rally domestic and international support.

Propaganda techniques, on the other hand, are employed to manipulate emotions, incite fear, and demonize the enemy. In the Yemen Civil War, both Iran and Saudi Arabia have resorted to such techniques to sway public sentiment in their favor. These techniques may include the use of inflammatory language, selective reporting, and the portrayal of one's own actions as defensive while framing the enemy's actions as aggressive.

The impact of disinformation campaigns and propaganda techniques in the Yemen conflict cannot be overstated. Such tactics not only fuel the sectarian divide but also deepen the polarization within Yemeni society. They undermine trust, impede dialogue, and hinder efforts towards a negotiated settlement. Moreover, the international community's response to the conflict is often influenced by the narratives presented through these campaigns, leading to further complications in resolving the crisis.

Diplomats and politicians must recognize the role of disinformation campaigns and propaganda techniques in the Yemen Civil War. They must remain vigilant in analyzing and verifying information, fact-checking claims, and challenging false narratives. Additionally, efforts should be made to counter these campaigns through transparent and accurate reporting, promoting dialogue, and encouraging critical thinking among the public.

Ultimately, a negotiated settlement in the Yemen Civil War requires the dismantling of disinformation campaigns and the promotion of truthful and unbiased narratives. By exposing the tactics used by regional powers and non-state actors, diplomats and politicians can contribute to a more informed approach towards resolving the conflict. Only through a comprehensive understanding of the challenges posed by disinformation and propaganda can sustainable peace and stability be achieved in Yemen.

Chapter 11: The Potential for a Negotiated Settlement in the Yemen Civil War

International Mediation Efforts and Peace Talks

In the midst of the devastating Yemen Civil War, international mediation efforts and peace talks have emerged as a glimmer of hope in the pursuit of stability and resolution. The conflict, which has been widely recognized as a proxy war between Iran and Saudi Arabia, has attracted the attention of diplomats and politicians from around the world who are eager to find a peaceful solution to the ongoing crisis.

Regional powers, such as the United States, the United Kingdom, and the United Nations, have played a crucial role in facilitating and mediating peace talks between the warring parties. These efforts have aimed to address the root causes of the conflict, including the impact of sectarianism and religious ideologies, and to foster a negotiated settlement that can bring an end to the suffering of the Yemeni people.

The international community's response to the Yemen Civil War has been multifaceted. While some countries have provided military support to one side or the other, others have focused on humanitarian aid and diplomatic initiatives to promote peace. The humanitarian crisis caused by the war has been a major concern, with millions of Yemenis facing famine, disease, and displacement. International actors have worked to provide essential aid and support to alleviate the suffering of the Yemeni people.

Non-state actors have also played a significant role in the Yemen Civil War. Groups such as the Houthis, who are backed by Iran, and various factions supported by Saudi Arabia, have complicated the conflict and made it even more difficult to reach a negotiated settlement. Understanding the dynamics of this proxy war and the influence of non-state actors is crucial for diplomats and politicians seeking to broker peace in Yemen.

In addition to the humanitarian crisis, the Yemen conflict has had severe economic consequences for the country. The destruction of infrastructure, collapse of the economy, and the disruption of vital industries such as agriculture and oil have exacerbated the suffering of the Yemeni people. International mediation efforts must take into account the economic aspects of the conflict and work towards a sustainable solution that can help rebuild Yemen's economy.

Furthermore, media coverage and propaganda have played a significant role in shaping the perception and understanding of the Yemen Civil War. Different actors have sought to manipulate public opinion to gain support for their respective causes. Diplomats and politicians need to be aware of these dynamics and work towards unbiased reporting and analysis to facilitate a fair and balanced negotiation process.

Despite the challenges and complexities, there is still potential for a negotiated settlement in the Yemen Civil War. International mediation efforts and peace talks provide an opportunity for all parties involved to find common ground and work towards a lasting solution. Diplomats and politicians must continue to engage with the conflict, understanding the proxy war dynamics between Iran and Saudi Arabia, and the impact of sectarianism and religious ideologies, to pave the way for a peaceful and prosperous Yemen.

Challenges and Prospects for a Sustainable Peace Agreement

In the midst of the devastating Yemen Civil War, diplomats and politicians face numerous challenges in their pursuit of a sustainable peace agreement. This subchapter delves into the complex dynamics that have contributed to the conflict, exploring the role of regional powers, the impact of sectarianism, the international community's response, the humanitarian crisis, non-state actors, economic consequences, proxy war dynamics, religious ideologies, media coverage, and the potential for a negotiated settlement.

The Yemen Civil War is a proxy war between Iran and Saudi Arabia, with both regional powers vying for influence in the Middle East. The subchapter examines how their involvement has exacerbated the conflict, prolonging the suffering of the Yemeni people and hindering efforts to achieve a lasting peace.

Sectarianism has played a significant role in fueling the Yemen conflict, as different religious and ethnic groups have become embroiled in the fighting. The subchapter explores the impact of sectarian tensions and how they have further complicated efforts to find a resolution.

The international community's response to the Yemen Civil War has been mixed, with some countries providing support to the warring factions while others push for a peaceful resolution. The subchapter analyzes the various approaches taken by different nations and the implications of their actions on the prospects for peace.

The ongoing war has created a dire humanitarian crisis in Yemen, with millions of people in need of assistance. The subchapter highlights the devastating consequences of the conflict on the civilian population and the urgent need for humanitarian aid.

Non-state actors, such as militias and terrorist groups, have also played a significant role in the Yemen Civil War. The subchapter examines their motivations and actions, and how their involvement further complicates the path to peace.

Economically, the Yemen conflict has had far-reaching consequences, with infrastructure destroyed and the economy in shambles. The subchapter explores the economic impact of the war and its implications for post-conflict recovery.

Propaganda and media coverage have also influenced the course of the Yemen conflict. The subchapter examines the role of media in shaping public opinion and the challenges it poses to achieving a negotiated settlement.

Despite the immense challenges, there is still potential for a negotiated settlement in the Yemen Civil War. The subchapter explores the prospects for peace, including the role of mediation efforts, the importance of inclusive dialogue, and the necessity of addressing the underlying grievances fueling the conflict.

In conclusion, the challenges and prospects for a sustainable peace agreement in the Yemen Civil War are multifaceted and complex. Diplomats and politicians must navigate the intricate dynamics of regional powers, sectarian tensions, humanitarian crises, non-state actors, economic consequences, propaganda, and media coverage. Despite these challenges, there is hope for a negotiated settlement that can bring an end to the suffering of the Yemeni people and pave the way for a more stable and prosperous future.

Conclusion: A Call for Diplomatic Solutions in the Yemen Conflict

In examining the complex dynamics of the Yemen Conflict, it becomes evident that a resolution cannot be achieved through military means alone. The proxy war between Iran and Saudi Arabia has turned Yemen into a battleground, with devastating consequences for its people. As diplomats and politicians, it is our responsibility to advocate for diplomatic solutions that prioritize the well-being of the Yemeni people and bring an end to this protracted conflict.

The role of regional powers in the Yemen Civil War has only exacerbated the situation. Iran and Saudi Arabia's involvement has turned Yemen into a proxy war, fueling sectarian tensions and exacerbating the conflict. It is imperative that regional powers, including Iran and Saudi Arabia, engage in meaningful dialogue and work towards a diplomatic resolution that addresses the underlying causes of the conflict.

The international community's response to the Yemen Civil War has been insufficient, with limited efforts to broker a negotiated settlement. The humanitarian crisis in Yemen has reached catastrophic levels, with millions of people facing famine, disease, and displacement. It is crucial that the international community increases its efforts to provide humanitarian aid and support peace talks between the warring parties.

Non-state actors have also played a significant role in the Yemen Civil War, further complicating the conflict. Groups like the Houthis have capitalized on the power vacuum to gain control and perpetuate the violence. A comprehensive diplomatic solution must involve engaging with these non-state actors, addressing their grievances, and integrating them into the political process.

The economic consequences of the Yemen conflict have been devastating. The war has decimated Yemen's infrastructure, crippled its economy, and left millions unemployed and impoverished. Diplomatic solutions must prioritize rebuilding efforts, economic development, and providing sustainable livelihoods for the Yemeni people.

Religious ideologies have also played a divisive role in the Yemen Civil War. It is crucial to foster dialogue and promote tolerance to bridge sectarian divides and deescalate tensions. Diplomatic efforts should aim to promote inclusivity, religious freedom, and respect for diversity to foster long-term stability in Yemen.

Media coverage and propaganda have further fueled the conflict, perpetuating misinformation and exacerbating divisions.

Diplomats and politicians must work towards countering propaganda, promoting responsible journalism, and fostering an environment of transparency and accountability.

Ultimately, a negotiated settlement is the most viable path towards peace in Yemen. Diplomats and politicians must actively engage with all parties involved, including regional powers, non-state actors, and the international community, to facilitate meaningful dialogue and negotiations. A comprehensive diplomatic solution must address the root causes of the conflict, prioritize the well-being of the Yemeni people, and pave the way for a stable and prosperous future for Yemen. It is our duty to advocate for diplomatic solutions and tirelessly work towards ending the Yemen Conflict.